BD $10.00

STONE BLIND LOVE

STONE BLIND LOVE

Barry Callaghan

TORONTO
A Stoddart, Exile Editions Book
1988

This Edition is published by Exile Editions Ltd.,
69 Sullivan Street, Toronto, Ontario, Canada
M5T 1C2

Sales Distribution
General Publishing Co. Ltd.
30 Lesmill Road, Don Mills, Ontario M3B 2T6

Typeset in Stempel Garamond by CAPS & LOWER CASE
Designed by LOU LUCIANI

Cover painting, tusche on paper by CLAIRE WEISSMAN WILKS

ISBN 0-920428-81-9

CONTENTS

Ma poésie le coeur heurté
Ma poésie de cailloux chahutés

GASTON MIRON

You didn't hurt me when you left me,
I know the best of friends must part,
but when my mother left me,
that was the one that broke my heart.

JAMES COTTON

Only kind of love
Is stone blind love.

TOM WAITS

for George Yemec

Body and Soul

A stone
seminates itself
surmounted
by its shadow.

The Sleepwalker

The night they met
on a cruise
through the Thousand Islands,
he left a bruise on her neck
and his clarinet
under the bed.
She fell asleep
and woke up on her feet
so much in love
the heart behind her rib
had no cage,
ageless.
But the moon lay cracked open
on the floor,
a spot of blood in the yolk.
An old adage:
pain and pleasure are two bells,
if one sounds, the other knells.

Dew

He dreamed in her ear
of cranes and horses copulating
in the skewbald air.
They lay under paper lanterns
tying
dark to dark
in the garden,
and woke bare and drunk
and wet in the morning.
Turning leaves
in a marrow bed,
he made a crib
of stones for kindling,
drew his hand through the dense grass,
and touched her cheek with damp:
"Our world is dew," he said,
"and here comes the sun."

Restless Stones

East of the waterfront grain silos
he was sitting on a stone.
"It's one of Lilith's eggs,
the beaches are strewn with the misbegotten."
A pearl of milk
on his lip was a fever sore.
"Stones never sleep, they grow,
they crawl up your legs,
the seeds
of all your misdeeds
until
you stand at last
with a stone
in each fist,
an enclosing wall your only
defense."

The Wall

They were two rooms sending precise messages:
one tap, two stars – falling star, shooting star,
and half-asleep heard
loose plaster fall inside the wall:
"Was that you, did you cough?"

She wrote in block letters:
"Without you I am lost,
I've no one to be silent with."
He answered in letters that writhed around each other
and she cried:

"Translate, translate."
He replied, "I love … you love."
She closed her eyes.
"No, not that word,
it has too many endings."

So every morning they began
at the beginning
until she said,
"Let us agree to disagree,"
a curse they could live with,
face to the wall, back to the wall.

In His Fever (1)

"Blood on my palms,
bits of bones, of fingers crossed,

of chairs, the brittle collapse
of movie break-away furniture
in the threadbare light of late autumn,

cut chrysanthemum leaves wilting
above the radiator like men
at the end of their rope, dancing,

all these flashing pieces
now my bright and broken world.

I don't dance, only by myself
in the dark, the way
your mother sings in the shower."

Somewhere There's Music

"Wearing an old engineer's cap
and worn sneakers,
your father would hitch-hike around town
so he could feel at home,
full of cranky talk,
intimate as hell
so long as he could say
he was a stranger,

his eyes
turning to tarnished silver
in the sunlight.
You couldn't see into him,
you just got this
lustre.
'I'm only passing through,'
he'd say and crack jokes,

and then on the outskirts at a Texaco
he'd clamber down
from a trucker's cab:
'Think I'll rest my bones a while.'
He'd walk all the way home, whistling,
to sit on the porch at night
and play his clarinet,
how high the moon

poking at me about how a man
always poaches on a woman,
taking
quail and quim
he called it and laughed,
like there was no denying
the distress he'd done,
but he always lied.

All he ever took from anyone
was a free ride,
pretending
he'd never been born
here
so maybe
he'd never have to
die."

In His Fever (2)

"When I am alone I think of dying.
I am most alone when I sleep.
I cannot sleep,
each sound boring
through still black water
inside my brain,
a silt of severed notes,
roe of the Darktown Queen
row row your boat gently
down the stream
I never dream. I hear
men hauling their ashes
among hookers,
sloe-eyed
on borrowed time,
loan sharks upstream
licking their chops.
The sun is hiding out
in the trout's eye,
I see nothing.
Only trees,
water-logged
piano keys: white and black,
without leaves, no sound, no sun,
cosy oblivion.
Some men
count their toes.
Eleven. One extra.
My son.
The trees are long grey drums,
their emptiness shines
a black light
merrily,
merrily, life is but a dream."

Now It Will Rain

In the dry heat,
when the grass yellowed and the garden caked,
two men brought a wooden barrel
packed with ice
to the back porch.

Father,
wearing long black rubber gloves,
hauled fish out of the crushed ice,
wrapping each silver corpse
in old newsprint.

The ice melted,
leaving the barrel half full of briny water.
"Never be short-sighted,"
he said,
staring down into the black pool
vanishing in the heat.
"Look to the salt ring
left around the inside, the residue."

At night, during the second week,
he kept watch, waiting,
and when the full moon appeared in the water
he clapped the lid across the barrel mouth.
"Now," he said, "we have caught
the moon in a ring,
now it will rain."

The clouds in the night sky
were the dark of his eyes.

The Queen Of Heaven

On summer days
mother took a bottle of rainwater
down into the basement
to sit among empty seedling trays.
It was cool close to the wall.
There were small dunes
of carpenter ant dust
in the corners.
"They say a stillborn child
was buried under here before our time,
wrapped in a blanket,
before we built the house,
before father drowned."
She sat in an old white wicker lawn chair
and sipped her water.
"The child's in concrete now,
but he talks to me,
discretely,
of fields of flowers
balmy with the blue of the moon.
I can feel the sky full of stars at my feet."

Pilgrim Stone

We'll root this cellar out of the earth,
hoist it overhead, a skycage for birds,
or turn a skein of sky-blue smoke
into umber peat,
or a cranberry. Who could quarrel with that?

No stone is static, or perpetual.
I saw stone climb a tower,
it braided a nest among black crows,
and hatched dappled stones, fledglings.
Who later learned to fly.
Why should pilgrim stones
in the sky dazzle your eye?

O spring is myrtle green,
and back from warmer climes,
pilgrim stone sings in the birch by the cage.
Sings its flight, charmed,
sings flight.

Horses

Stones, like horses, hunger for a woman
and sprout wings.
They stamp their moon-shaped hoofs,
leaving behind wells
of aloneness

and, each brain a roistering clew,
gallop headlong
off a cliff. They roger the wind
with golden falchions,
bite huge teeth

into the clouds.
Their wingbeat pains,
the dark scoops out their eyes. They fall
through the air,
through the sea, tumble

and rasp along the floor till
the last nub of bone
is worn down. Disgorged
on the shore, they are bolls
of unbridled lust.

Zeus & Sons

Stones lose their wings
and lie
in common ground,
wear a crown of earth.
Men
spill common seed,
dream their sons as stars
and never die.

The Diviner

The foundation was wet,
small pools settled
on the cellar floor.
A witcher
wearing a dung-crusted cap
circled the house
criss-crossing his track.
The willow he held whipped down,
bark tore in his hands.

"There's a crick on the corner below:
whatever's ripe to know
rips the flesh."
He stood buttoning
and unbuttoning his plaid mackinaw,
little beads of sweat
in his blonde moustache,
and then he pointed to the roofless
stone school house
along the road,
a shell for flying squirrels.

"Ten years ago
we dug up a child's grave,
sewn into a blanket,

the skull so thin you could see the sun
through the crown."
He scraped the instep of his shoe clean
with the witching stick
and ducked his head
as if he felt the flap of a wing
or a chill wind
on his neck.

"Around here the dead come to light
in the damndest ways,"
he said and turned away
toward his truck
parked by the roadside.
After a blinding snow storm
he had found his wife
swimming for home
in a snow bank.

In Her Marrow

"When dark sucks
all the light
out of rock
and I am dead,
I want no headstone.
Marry fire
to the flame in my marrow
and let me end
as
I began:
ash among the ashlings,
boneless
in
God's brainpan as he speaks
and the sun falls
out of his
mouth."

Phoenix

Ivarr the Boneless,
bivouacked on the shore
of the Salt Sea,
pocketed a small stone
and warmed it in his hand
all the way home
to Ringworm,
a garrison
south
of the Great Wall.

In a fit of anger
he had the stone sewn
into the mouth
of a spy,
the body beheaded,
burned,
and the face with its pursed mouth
fired
from a catapult
into the Dark Wood

where it was found
by a blonde horseman,
his breast painted blue,
who hung the head
by the hair over his hearth,
waiting for it to speak.
The thread dried,
broke,
and the stone leapt out
into the mulberry pit.

He raked the coals
until the stone
cracked.
A black serpent
stood
in the flame: –
flute,
flowering stem,
the hooded priest's
backbone,

coiling
into a bracelet of
ash,
a name in smoke,
Ivarr the Boneless,
and wearing a winged helmet
he rode to the Salt Sea
to redeem the world
by war if
needs be.

A Wound Of Light

Two soldiers protecting tourists
from homeless children
running loose in the streets
cradled their guns as a young man
with reddish hair
knelt in the sun
and pulled a stem
of ragweed
from between the paving stones.
"Christ was only an acrobat," he said, "reaching
for what was not there,
his Father's forgiveness,
but if Jesus could try to pray,
then why not me?
He left this world lunatic with the despair
of millions at prayer,
watching by night for angels
in parachutes.
But only spiders fill the air
with their nets
and I hear
the clack clack clacking
of a blind man's cane.
It is my heart.
I can see the bones in my hand,
pink, with petals
in the branches of all the veins.
The torn root
I hold
is
a wound of light,
a flower for the unforgiving."

In His Fever (3)

"Pain is a habit,
an impaling flower,
and she was in full bloom
weeding
the circle of silence
around
a broken stone.
She was in no hurry,

but tilted drunk,
I rode a broomstick horse
through stoplights
stalking
the cry inside a cry,
the syllable
in
a serpent's egg
that
might rectify."

What Does Darkness Know?

"What does darkness know
that I don't?
Your father fell in love
with the seed-
pearl light
in a mulatto singer's
eyes.

She turned him on the wheel
of her tambourine,
tore
her clothes
and dreamed me dead.
The moon
had him by the horn.

But when you lie down
with a woman's
dream
that you despise,
the air gets thin,
you wake
with dry leaves in your hair.

He came home,
lips
the color of slate
and crouched
like a convict
inside
the cell of his bones,

breaking rocks and slurping water
from a tin cup,
spilling more than he swallowed
into the gravel between his thighs."

Window In The Water

Alone with herself
she would sit in candlelight,
her sleeves stained by wax,
and play the shadows
of her hands
like charred wings on the wall.
"Your father played a black flute
with silver stops
and told me I was the silence
between notes.
There wasn't a cloud in the sky
when he drowned,
only a thousand thousand
windows in the water.
He opened one
and went out into the dark."

In His Fever (4)

"There's an unhinged stealth
in the pimp-walking dudes
who crowd the bars
to hear me play,
breaking loose and free-basing
a dream of love unlocked
by the minor key
of the moon
trailing
black notes.
They prowl the gaps
between
spite and tears,
my clarinet
their
periscope."

Medusa Among The Moochers

"If love is where the heart be,
baby, I got a pawnshop heart
full of clefs and sharps,
so when you start with me
gird up your loins
and count your coin.
Snakes and Ladders
is my game,
the adder's
kiss
a Stairway to the Stars.
AC-DC,
S & M
(beat me daddy eight to the bar),
or
All Around The World –
life is only a boatride
and curbside is where you decide
on who's to help you hide
your fears in the land of tears.
But before you is quick, jack, be nimble.
Check the chicks
for needle marks between their knuckles,
keep an eye peeled for their muscle.
Them pimps'll jump on your head
and shit in your hair.
The cops will fingerprint your prayers.
But I'll carry you safe home

to the other side,
alive with little love bites
till you're so high you'll shed your skin
and swear you're dead.
When I get my wig hat on,
I give great head.
Never mind
those moochers you leave behind,
worrying whether they're
with or without sin,
or the stones they is casting,
warning you to atone.
If we get eye to eye
I turn them
to stone."

As She Sang

She carried a handfull of pebbles
in her pocket
and wore a silver locket
at her throat.
"I loved your father more than any man,
but he made light
of me
and touched the darkness
in my heart,
so I cut his hair
while he slept
and before he died he stood
in this field and wept.
His tears
turned to stones."
She cast seven pebbles from her pocket
and each, striking a stone,
struck a note,
finding a melody
so soulful
she mimed his weeping
as she sang.

Mirror Mirror

The devil
dances in our eye,
creature
of our own creation.
And God,
also
in the image of the race,
wears our face.
The sorrow
is,
the devil knows
we live in his skin
but God
cannot believe
how much
we love him.

And So To Bed

God, in a word, was light.
Adam, in deed, was dark,
the silhouette
of Himself.
Eve, for a lark,
split
the syllable,
and did a dance
under the rib of death
that left Adam,
already out a bone, out of breath.
"God is a bore," she cried.
"At least you're his dark side."
When they refused to atone
God shed a single tear,
a stone, and said,
"Out you go, you'd be better off dead."
Bereft, abandoned
of all hope
(Eve was busy birthing in her bed),
Adam tried another tree
and a rope,
anchoring his feet
with the tear
to get the job done,
but then he saw
a second Adam,
god in another guise

on a far hill.
Adam looked into his face,
into his eyes.
"Imitation has the grace of flattery,"
he said, feeling wise.
He climbed down from his tree,
cast the tear in the sea.
"It gave me a strange thrill,"
he told Eve,
"seeing him dead, almost sexual,
as he hung himself
in my stead."
She rolled her eyes.
"Heresies come, heresies go,
but thank god for small mercies,
you're alive,"
and she brought him to bed.

Bread Alone

The back of the stone
does not know you,
but the hollow
it makes in the earth for your head
knows you.
Lie down there
and listen to the leaves
of Adam's tree catch at the wind,
but bear in mind,
if
the sigh for air
that gives happiness
its haunting tone
of distress
becomes despair,
when you lie down dead
the stone put
in your mouth will be your only
bread.

The Glass Heart

On Sunday mornings
mother still made ginger snap cookies,
little brown girls on the run
with seed-pearl eyes,
and then she sat cleaning
her silver forks and knives
with a chamois cloth.
"Your father was crazy as a bag of hammers:
long after we quit
making love,
he wanted to undress my brain
because he couldn't understand
my laughter,
but laughter is glass
and has bones
that can be broken,
not by sticks and stones
but by names
that break your heart."

Not Me, Demosthenes

Beside a pallisade
covered with wisteria
a doctor wearing a hearing aid
stood over their son in army fatigues.
He had slit his wrists,
the cuts were healing.
"I saw a white hawk," he said,
"who had lock-jaw.
Clap hands. Clap hands, the burning
cigarettes around my bed
are campfires in the hills.
Someone persists."
He plucked
a petal from a flower
and blew it off his finger.
"Just like a kiss,"
their son said as it fell.
"Some guys sleep their death.
Some guys do what they're told.
Hup two three four.
Some guys kill them young and old.
I won't fight.
Some guys stand on the shore,
mouths full of stones
speaking above the sea.
Not me. How crazy can you be?"

Homesick

She knelt
beside her carved satinwood bed,
clearing out
a cedar hope chest.

"Years ago I looked into the palm
of my hand
and saw the life line
disappearing.

I closed my fist
and held on to what I had."
She laid a tortoise shell hair clasp on the coverlet
beside a lilac sachet,

and then elbow-length kid gloves,
a rhinestone choker
and ebony chopsticks inlaid with jade,
a glass ball

thick with falling snow
and capsules of holy water
ordered by mail
but never opened.

"Homesick in my own house,
I limped out of your father's life
while lying in his bed
looking for a cure.

He was smarter.
He held on to nothing, spent money like water
and washed
his hands of my world."

Water Music

I

The dance in water
is light
but
start from the dark
where spillage
gathers

sing water
sing light
sing
as water
seeds a cloudburst
to come

sing the worst
the failing light
but learn
the soothfastness
of stone
shrouded in rain

joy
is the stillness
in what's done
as day burns
and becomes
again
the dance in water
that is
light.

II

In the trout's discus eye
the crawfish
is king of silt,
prone
among shells the shape of sleep.
Drills of light
through
the overhanging harness
of lily roots:
swallow water, swallow light,
an old trout
settles on the bottom stones
out of sight.

III

Pond dusted with pollen,
light beading a line:
a frog hooked
through
the throat
flexes his legs.
Where wind and water meet,
halo after halo
widens as water spiders
rehearse the last dance.

IV

Water wears down stone.
Black stone, a black
pebble, syllable of pitch
and toss, the charred
light of lost speech.

Singe the air with rain-
bows. A single word
is light to the serpent in stone.
A sentence swallows its tail,
wheel within a wheel, rolling.

Along The Amazon

"No one sane sleeps
in the chrome light of 5 AM's calm,
not with trip wires along the shore
where I found the relic,
the jawbone of his word, broken.
Because I am not going to die
I let the hooded hangman
hold me in his arms,
rope me to a tree,
and laughed,
but not the heart hunter
with his poisoned dart,
his necklace
of shrunken
loves."

Eurydice Descending

At dusk, as the light dropped,
she followed a dogwood trail
behind the house into the ravine,
ducking under poplar branches
stripped clean inside
the hanging cocoons of tent caterpillars,
skirting a mound of bristle and maggot,
a decaying raccoon,
until she reached brushes and eelgrass,
a cove of slate grey water.
She undressed and slid
down a stone shelf
into the shallows,
dragging shore-slime and fronds,
and splashed cold water over her belly and breasts,
staring at the sky
moth eaten by light, pale stars.
She eased into the slough.
It had the feel of ointment
as she scissored down
to the braided roots on the bottom,
eyes closed, ears singing,
the voice of her drowned man
filling her lungs, swelling,
until the sound became a searing light
behind her eyes
that drove her crashing
into the air,
gulping down the dark
as she crawled ashore.

Hollow In The Heart

Mother sat in church
with confetti in her grey hair,
beating his tin cup on the pew.
"Pluck your eye, pluck your eye," she cried.
"In the land of the blind
the one-eyed
man is king.
Try to read
your mind
before you lose it."

She rubbed the dented cup
on her sleeve
and looked for her face in the shine.
"What's in here," she said,
holding her head in her hand,
"is blind love.
I start each day by swallowing a small stone,
not seeking to atone
for sins, but only to fill the hollow
in my heart."

She scissored folded sheets of music,
set the paper snowflakes
on fire in a dry font.
"Ash is evidence
of the sacrifice
we make,
absence of water
the pain
in which we partake."

To Meet A Stone

I

Skirt a ravine
meet a stone
the sideling stone
a crony

on either side
set stones
and stay inside

then show a single
stone the soil
transplant
plant

weed and hoe
weed and water
the single stone

till it moans
till it glistens
and
a flower erupts
in the core

hardening blossoms
begin to
peel

as bees
sheath the blossom
with more water

as fruit evolves
oscillating the head
bracing

as the fruit's
freshening air grows
ticklish
seeds
grow
dusty

touch the heart
task the heart

and survive
by taking stone's
heavy seeds
to heart.

II

Coils compressed in stone – my sleepless stone.
Unsprung coils in stone – my sleepless stone.

Not riverbottom of redfins, nor
seaweed, nor the apple core's worm – no one sleeps.

Stone gathering – day in, day out.
Stones sprout inward – day in, day out.

Outbound bird, smoke
outbound, but not you.

No other escape, escape is inscape.
No other wit, only inwit.

Winsome as a wagtail flying
inward – so stone flies.

III

Let's not discuss stone.
Not a word. Stone is holy.
Watch a grey stone rise over the hill,
as others see the sun rise.

A gray stone? And up there,
as the clock strikes twelve?
Yes, stone mounts our sky,
as others track the circling sun.

IV

Stone speech
isn't mangled at all
sound asleep under water
it will rise

stand for hours
listening by the waterfront
for one single
stone word.

Sesephus The Stone King

"Git down, git down,
you got to git down
on your hands and knees
and keep your ear close to the ground.
There are druggies
who honey-dip around parking lots
playing the clown
instead of the clarinet,
looking for
peddlers of high renown
as in H,
or dealers doing sap of the moon plant,
crack and smack.
I used to dial a vial
myself,
a little digital digitalis,
the speed I dropped
absorbing the absence
in the air
with a light so rare
it baked
the shadow of despair
on a wall that wasn't there.
God almighty, it was a time
in fields of asphodel.

Now I got to keep my head clear,
my nose clean,
and all my seed inside a dark clock.
This is quarry country,
the bunsen burner
is holy fire and funeral pyre,
the only begotten son
is dumb, deaf, crippled
and blind,
a forgotten runner
in the mind of godfathers,
all those old trouts
who got the lock
on the chemical combinations,
XYZ down to a T,
the seeds of obloquy and obscurity.
I was in their graces,
and they put me through the paces,
warned me to never leave no traces
of the knowledge I knew.
Called me the King of Crack.

But I put on my eye-patch
and pranced uptown
and came unlatched
playing pin-ball with the sun.
Broke the trust
and left a trail of angel dust
so wide you'd swear
a snail had crossed
my nerves.
Too late, I clapped a coin
under my tongue,
played dead among the misbegotten,
but they hung me out on this fire escape
where coming down
is worse than being bung-holed,
not just gored but gutted
by the privation
of salvation.
It's all up hill from here on in.
I got this shameless stone,
a dead sun,
inside my brain,
a curse I roll toward
a relief only the condemned thief
could understand
a long way east of Eden.

Over the brow of the hill
the gods are at play.
Your father, mine.
It's never night,
always day as they lie,
cheat, vilify,
and replete with codes and codicills
pop a pill and change their shills to toads.
Your father, mine.
The gods got no shame,
so who's to blame for the stone
inside my brain?
They complain I broke a trust. Haw!
Roll on, baby, roll.
The stone don't constitute no pain.
What's terrifying is the gods will come again,
and the narcs, too,
taking a leg, a hand,
they is all sharks."

Heaven's Gate

A single flame
is the eye
of the
needle
through which
lovers
must
pass
in the dreaming
skulls
of
the unloved
planted
as milestones
along the road
toward
home.

Le Petit Mort

In her last year,
she lay awake all night,
hands folded on her breast,
an enforced calm,
waiting for seams
of light between the shades
so she could slip downstairs
to her horsehair chair
and sleep,
whimpering in refusal of a dream,
waking in a sweat
at noon.

"Sane, sane," she said,
sipping jasmine tea spiked with gin,
"we're all insane.
I undo my nightmares
and find
the chalk light that came
into his eyes
when he was afraid
of freedom.
It's the light a woman sees
when a man dies a little
with the pain
of a
pleasure
he cannot sustain
in her."

In His Fever (5)

"Condemned to half light,
we want clemency,
but there is no charge, only conviction.
Twelve bells
on our carousel.
Twelve bells.
Though the world's unwell,
blouse and shirt undone, barefoot,
we drag the narrows of our dreams
grappling for a future,
upend the clock
in a circle
of calendar stones
and lope for miles across our room
planting kisses on the walls.
Dancing keeps the vermin down
and it rains.
But the moon caroms off the water
and comes to rest
on our bed,
a crystal ball
filled with ash."

Grace

The light
inside
a
stone
is
like a dream
refusing
to be
revealed
or
the voice
of
God
concealed
in
the heart.

Au Revoir

Mother On Her Death Bed.

I

"I'm here, afloat in clear water,
drifting between white elms,
god's voice is the sound of snow,
his scorn the color of water.
Who painted my toe-nails red,
another woman in our lives,
the taunt of her kindness?
Yesterday, pinned to the chair by sunlight
I had a premonition. Of rue,
not remorse, but rue.
Turning in the shallows of the river
like a child's toy top
painted with a clown's
face in the flowers,
that insistent hum
of all the little holes in our lives
tuned to a stagnant note
as snow falls
melting in the water."

II

“A gull on the sullied air,
wind in his sleeve.
City gulls. Water birds
without water
skidding belly-first
into the pond of heat-light
on a paved lot.
For years I felt I had no periphery.
Now I’m peripheral at the core.
As children we blew bird nests apart
with a water hose.
I’m old,
cut the bone of my arm
and count the rings.
I see a pelican pecking its own breast,
feeding the young its blood.
Birds cramp my dreams,
they keep crashing.
I’ll say goodbye
though a mother only means goodbye
when you meet again.”

On Her Death

Broken water
in an agate glass,
through
the needle's eye,
a star.
The earth at her mouth
is grass,
her dust transmutes
to this music.

Au Revoir, *Grace*, *Now It Will Rain*, *Bread Alone*, *On The Death of His Mother*, *Mirror Mirror*, *The Queen Of Heaven* and *Sleepwalker* appeared in *Toronto Life*.

The Sleepwalker, *Dew*, *In Her Marrow*, *Window In The Water*, *The Glass Heart*, *Homesick*, *Hollow In The Heart*, and *Le Petit Mort* appeared in *The Ontario Review*, Princeton.

As translated by Robert Marteau, *Sisyphe le roi pétrifié*, *Grâce*, *Pierres turbulentes*, *Il va pleuvoir*, *La reine des cieux*, *Une blessure de lumière*, *En chantant*, *Pas moi*, *Démosthène*, and *Un creux au coeur* appeared in *Po&sie*, Paris.

Eurydice Descending, *The Queen of Heaven*, and *Window In The Water* appeared in *Prospice*, Stoke-on-Trent.

NOTES

I began these poems in April of 1987 on Abu Tor, across the vale of Gihone from the old stone walls of Jerusalem. Back home in July, I sometimes drove to the race track in the afternoon listening to Tom Waits sing about derelicts and derelictions, stone blind love. His song went one way, mine another. Such is racing.

Body and Soul is translated from the Serbian of Miodrag Pavlović. *Pilgrim Stone* and *To Meet A Stone* are translated from the Latvian of Imants Ziedonis.

Ivarr the Boneless was a Danish adversary of Alfred the Great.

Bread Alone: the first two lines are a translation from Garcia Lorca.

The Sleepwalker and *Now It Will Rain* are dedicated to John Montague on his sixtieth birthday.

Medusa Among The Moochers is dedicated to Seán Virgo who let these stones crawl up his legs.

Heaven's Gate is dedicated to Miodrag Pavlović.

Books By Barry Callaghan

POETRY

The Hogg Poems And Drawings
As Close As We Came
Stone Blind Love

FICTION

The Black Queen Stories

TRANSLATIONS

Atlante (Robert Marteau)
Treatise On White And Tincture (Robert Marteau)
Interlude (Robert Marteau)
Singing At The Whirlpool (Miodrag Pavlović)
A Voice Locked In Stone (Miodrag Pavlović)
Fragile Moments (Jacques Brault)
Flowers Of Ice (Imants Ziedonis)